*optional 8va to m. 55

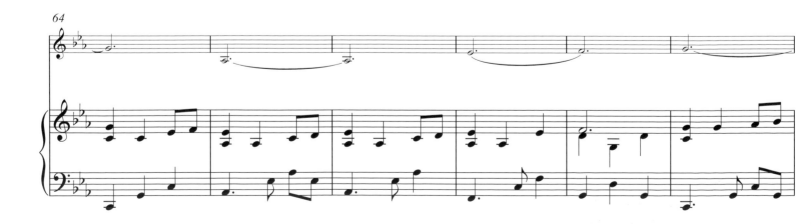

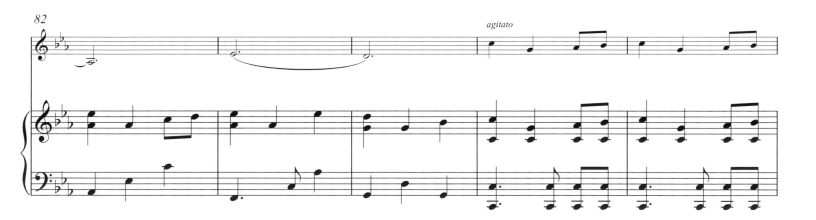

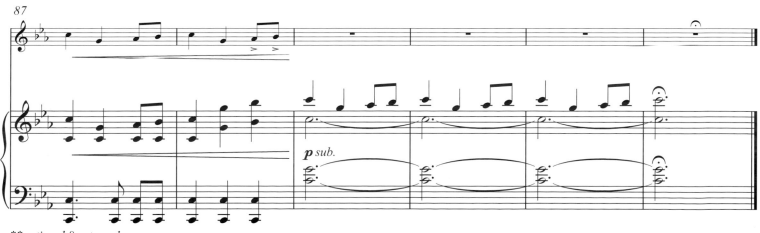

**optional 8va to end

GAME OF THRONES

Theme from the HBO Series

VIOLIN

By RAMIN DJAWADI

*optional 8va to m. 55
**optional 8va to end

Also available:

BEAUTY & THE BEAST MEDLEY – arr. Lindsey Stirling
Violin/Piano 00238143 $9.99

DISNEY SONGS FOR SOLO VIOLIN & PIANO
Violin/Piano 00159561 $19.99

HALLELUJAH – arr. Lindsey Stirling
Violin/Piano 00250149 $8.99

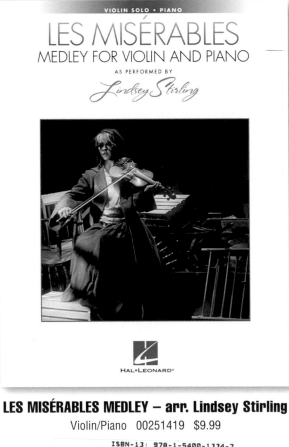

LES MISÉRABLES MEDLEY – arr. Lindsey Stirling
Violin/Piano 00251419 $9.99

ISBN-13: 978-1-5400-1334-7
Distributed By

HAL LEONARD
00253399   9 781540 013347

HL00253399

8 88680 71918 0

Visit Hal Leonard Online at
www.halleonard.com

U.S. $7.99

GAME OF THRONES

THEME FROM THE HBO SERIES
MUSIC BY RAMIN DJAWADI

UNIVERSAL

UNIVERSAL MUSIC
PUBLISHING GROUP
www.universalmusicpublishing.com

EXCLUSIVELY DISTRIBUTED BY

HAL•LEONARD®

7777 W. BLUEMOUND RD. P.O. BOX 13819
MILWAUKEE, WISCONSIN 53213

GAME OF THRONES
Theme from the HBO Series

By RAMIN DJAWADI

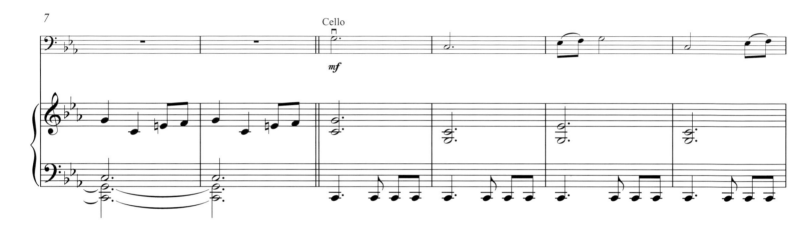